The
Meditation
Journal

The Meditation Journal

28 Spiritual Growth Exercises
to Inspire Inner Peace,
Self-Awareness, and Happiness

*Mary Sheldon
and Christopher Stone*

DOVE
BOOKS

ISBN 0-7871-0740-9

Printed in the United States of America

Dove Books
8955 Beverly Boulevard
West Hollywood, CA 90048

Distributed by Penguin USA

Jacket and text design and layout by Mauna Eichner
Cover illustration by Tanya Maiboroda

First Printing: May 1996

10 9 8 7 6 5 4 3 2 1

For Bob—
all the good karma I've ever earned,
wrapped up into one adorable husband.

M.S.

For My Parents, Elsie and Phil Di Leo—
with great affection, love, and respect.

C.S.

Acknowledgments

Writing this book has been a long-time dream of mine. Thank you, Michael Viner and Deborah Raffin Viner, for giving Christopher and me the opportunity.

Loving Thanks also to my precious family and friends.

And thank you to all those teachers and writers who keep the Light so bright.

Mary Sheldon

Thank you, God, for allowing the healing that made it possible for me to write again.

Thank you, Mary Sheldon, for dropping this wonderful project in my lap.

Thank you, Sidney and Alexandra Sheldon, for your very special help.

Thank you, Dr. Michael Hall, for your healing treatments.

Thank you, Jose Garcia, Jr., for all your support.

Thank you, David Stoebner, for your unflagging devotion.

And thanks to each and every one who prayed for my recovery.

Christopher Stone

Contents

Introduction   xiii

PART I
The Exercises

	The Relaxation Technique	2
1	Accepting Yourself	4
2	The Five-Point Star	8
3	Your Heart's Desire	12
4	Your Inner Child	18
5	Forgiveness	26
6	Prosperity	30
7	Changing Chairs	34
8	Kindness Day	40
9	Your Probable Self	48

10	Love Letter	54
11	When You Wish Upon Yourself	62
12	Your Relationships	70
13	Get Out of That Rut	76
14	Affirmations	82
15	To Your Health	96
16	The Time Machine	100
17	Thinking for Yourself	106
18	Releasing Your Feelings	112
19	Counting Your Blessings	116
20	Meeting Your Guide	124
21	Releasing Unhappiness and Accepting Joy	130
22	The Fork in the Road	134
23	Living in the Moment	140
24	Inner Voices	146
25	Last Moments	152
26	Past-Life Recall	158
27	World Peace	178
28	Affirmations Two	184

PART II

The Alternates

1	Dream Work	200
2	Telepathic Communication	208
3	The Spark	214
4	Five-Minute Pick-Me-Up	216
	Suggested Reading	218

Introduction

The Meditation Journal was first written for myself, to fill a need that I perceived in the rows and rows of metaphysical/self-help/counseling guides on bookstore shelves. I'm unashamedly addicted to these books—not only to their philosophical content, but also to the helpful exercises and meditations most of them include. Corners of particularly wise pages are assiduously turned over; favorite passages are feverishly underscored; xeroxed copies of best beloved meditations are stacked by my bedside. My file box overflows.

But after ten years of this, it's gotten bewildering. It's gotten chaotic. It's gotten to be too much. One could spend every moment trying to keep up with it all. Inner child exercises, past life regressions, affirmations, creative visualizations, expanding psychic awareness, and on and on. So many paths to go down, one branch leading to another, and there simply isn't time to go down all of them. Instead of being the life-enhancing practice I had hoped, my inner search was becoming just one more impossible task.

Not only that, but I disliked the haphazardness of it all. I'd do a little bit of work in this area, a little bit of work in that area, but there was no sense of progress, no organization, no way to keep track of what I was learning from month to month.

I found myself needing some sort of plan. On one hand, I wanted to do a variety of exercises, to taste as many metaphysical experiences as possible. On the other, I wanted to remain focused and feel a clear sense of growth as time went on.

What I needed, I decided, was a journal. Each day, for twenty-eight days, there would be a new and consciousness-expanding meditation or exercise to do. After I did it, there would be space to write down what I had learned from the experience. The following day I would go on to the next assignment. Then, after four weeks, I would find myself back at day one. As with a five-year diary, I would be able to see what I had written the month before, write a new entry for the present month, and be able to compare and chart my progress of self-awareness.

I couldn't find such a book, so I decided to make my own.

Here is where my friend Christopher Stone comes in. A gifted psychic, teacher, and the author of a wonderful self-help book entitled *Re-Creating Your Self,* Christopher has been my friend and metaphysical teacher for ten years. Together we have compiled the thirty-two exercises that compose this book: twenty-eight for the four weeks' work, and four alternates, in case a particular meditation simply doesn't suit on a particular day.

Some of the exercises we created are our own. Some are favorites we have culled from our reading and from seminars we've attended and refined for this book. Some are basically psychological in approach. Others border on the occult.

The object is not to embrace any one particular teaching or shoot for one specific goal, but rather to provide a smorgasbord for the soul—thirty-two different techniques to increase growth, self-awareness, and the expansion of consciousness.

This book is an adventure book. X marks the spot, and the spot is You. I hope this journal will help you find the hidden treasure inside.

Mary Sheldon
Los Angeles, California
April 1996

I have been writing since I was eight years old. I have been writing professionally for the past 25 years—plays, screenplays, nightclub acts, TV quiz show questions, magazine reviews and feature articles, books, etc. This project is among my very favorites—and it is my first work since surviving a near-fatal stroke last year. Thank you, Dove Books, for giving me the chance to work with my beloved Mary Sheldon for the first time in five years.

I have been doing exercises similar to these my entire adult life, and I have benefited greatly from them. A few of these exercises were once assignments for students in my psychic development classes. Two of these exercises were assignments for the Re-Creating Your Self course that I taught for several years for California State University Extended Education.

Like Mary Sheldon, my friend and co-author, it is also my hope that these exercises will be a smorgasbord for your spirit that will increase your sense of well-being, enhance your self-confidence, and expand your consciousness. If you are inclined to write, I would love to read about your personal experiences with our book.

Christopher Stone
Dallas, Texas
April 1996

PART I

The
Exercises

The Relaxation Technique

Before doing each of the exercises, we suggest you begin with a relaxation technique. The one below is adapted from an exercise in Christopher's book, *Re-Creating Your Self*. However, if you already have a technique you're comfortable with, by all means use that.

❧ ❧ ❧

Assume a comfortable position in a quiet, pleasant place; then close your eyes and begin.

Imagine that the muscles in your scalp and forehead are becoming very comfortable and relaxed. Your eyebrows relax, the area all around your eyes relaxes...the tiny muscles of your eyelids relax, and the relaxation continues to flow...

It spreads deep into the back of your throat, deep into your head and neck, deep into your shoulders...

Now your arms relax...first the upper arms, then the lower. You feel the relaxation spreading across the tops of your hands, sinking all the way through the palms, down the fingers…

Return your attention to your relaxed neck and shoulders. Let the relaxation flow into your chest and lungs. Your breathing becomes easy and gentle. Feel yourself becoming more deeply relaxed with each gentle breath. All outside sounds are unimportant.

Now let the relaxation spread deeply into your back. Feel it flow down to the small of your back, warming and loosening wherever it touches.

The relaxation spreads into your sides, your stomach. Feel the muscles of your stomach and hips relax.

And now your legs relax. The relaxation flows into your thighs and knees. Your calves relax, your ankles, your feet…the heels of your feet relax. And finally, even your toes relax.

Your entire body is at peace, and you remain perfectly aware and focused, ready for a new adventure.

$\mathcal{D}ay$

Accepting Yourself

TIME REQUIRED: *five minutes*

There is an old expression: "God has more goodness and mercy than a man could ever sin against." We could all use a little goodness and mercy, especially from ourselves. It's so easy to whip ourselves for our shortcomings and imperfections, and to save our unconditional love for when we're "perfect." What a waste. Give yourself a break. This exercise will help you embrace yourself as you are—at this moment—in all your glorious, fallible, bumbling, adorable humanity.

۰ ۰ ۰

1. Get comfortable, close your eyes, and do the relaxation exercise outlined earlier.

2. One at a time, list everything that you don't like about yourself—every trait you think could be improved, every mistake you feel you've ever made.

3. Announce each item out loud, and then add, *"and I love myself anyway!"* So you're twenty pounds

4

overweight? You love yourself anyway! So you got grumpy at your kid yesterday? You love yourself anyway! So you cheated on your eighth-grade math final? You love yourself anyway!

4. See yourself through God's eyes, as a human being who's doing his or her best and deserves to be loved, no matter what. Think of something special you can do for this wonderful piece of humanity that is you.

5. Write down your impressions of the experience in the space provided.

Month 1

_____

_____

_____

_____

_____

_____

_____

Month 2

_____

_____

Month 3

Month 4

Month 5

Month 6:

The Five-Point Star

TIME REQUIRED: *two minutes*

This is a very helpful exercise in strengthening your connection to the power of the Universe.

₀   ₀   ₀

1. Stand with your feet about two feet apart and your arms outstretched to the sides, shoulder height. Your body will form a five-point star. Close your eyes and take a few deep breaths.

2. Put your left hand palm up and your right hand palm down. Imagine a thin golden ray of pure healing light coming down from the heavens. See it entering your body through your upturned left palm. Imagine it circulating through your whole body, energizing and calming wherever it touches, and see it finally leaving through your downturned right palm.

3. Call to mind a particular situation or person in

your life that requires healing. Imagine shrinking that person or situation to only a few inches high. Now lovingly place that person or situation on the ground directly underneath your right palm.

4. See the golden light pouring down, flooding the person or situation with healing and blessing.

5. Take a few deep cleansing breaths and open your eyes. Write down your impressions of the experience in the space provided.

Month 1

_____

_____

_____

_____

_____

_____

_____

Month 2

_____

_____

Month 3

Month 4

10

Month 5

Month 6:

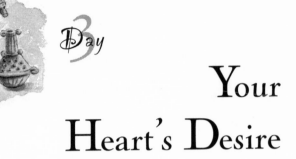

Day 3

Your Heart's Desire

TIME REQUIRED: *five to ten minutes*

This exercise is wonderful for programming the subconscious mind for success. The subconscious cannot distinguish between what is real and what is occurring in your imagination, so by doing this exercise you are laying down powerful groundwork for your dreams to come true.

o o o

1. Get comfortable, close your eyes, and do the relaxation exercise.

2. Think of your heart's desire. What is it? Is it your novel being published? Finding the perfect partner? A marvelous vacation? Radiant health? World peace? Whatever it is, focus on it. Now tell yourself that you've just gotten it.

3. Imagine what that would feel like. Make it as real to yourself as you can. Use all your powers of visualization. Use all your senses. Use all your passion.

See yourself surrounded by the people you love best. Hear them saying, "Congratulations! We knew you could do it!" Feel your own sense of wonderment and satisfaction.

Note: Have great fun with this exercise, but remember: The subconscious mind takes us literally at our word. The old adage, "Be careful what you wish for; you might get it," applies here.

Therefore, it's best not to get too specific in your visualization. If your dream is to be a champion high-diver, don't envision yourself winning the Olympic Gold Medal. Who knows? That may not be what's best for you in the long run. Similarly, if your dream is to be married to the perfect partner, don't go into this meditation with any particular person in mind. For all you know, the Universe may have a different, and better, mate in store for you.

Instead concentrate on a more general picture. Focus on the congratulations of loved ones and on your own feelings of happiness and success. Doing the meditation this way, your subconscious is jump-started to positive action, while at the same time the Universe has freedom to carry things out Its way.

4. Finish the exercise and take a few cleansing breaths. Write down your impressions of the experience in the space provided.

Month 1

_____
_____
_____
_____
_____
_____
_____
_____
_____
_____
_____
_____

Month 2

_____
_____
_____
_____
_____
_____

Month 3

Month 4

_____

_____

_____

_____

_____

_____

_____

_____

_____

_____

_____

_____

Month 5

_____

_____

_____

_____

_____

Month ☼:

Day 4

Your
Inner Child

TIME REQUIRED: *five to ten minutes*

We all have within us a wonderful character, a part of our psyche that is at once extremely vulnerable and extremely wise. This is our Inner Child, the symbol of the child we once were, and have probably long ago lost touch with. Getting in touch with that special part of ourselves can be very healing and rewarding, and this exercise is a helpful means to that end.

❂ ❂ ❂

1. Get comfortable, close your eyes, and do the relaxation exercise.

2. Imagine yourself in a favorite place where you feel at home and safe. Suddenly you feel a light tap on your shoulder. You turn, and there is your Inner Child. Is it a boy or a girl? What does he or she look like? How old is he or she? Does your Inner Child seem content, or upset and abandoned?

(*Note:* Since this Inner Child is symbolic, he or she will not necessarily look like you did as a child, or even be the same sex. For the rest of the exercise I will refer to the Inner Child as "she," for ease of reading.)

3. Hug your Inner Child. Reassure her that she is loved. Ask what she most needs to be happy. Ask what you can specifically do for her. Listen carefully to the answer.

4. Now ask your Inner Child what she can do for you. Ask what gift she has for you. What is the gift you are given? Why do you think it was given to you? When she gives you the gift, accept it gratefully.

5. Tell your Inner Child that she is cared for and safe, that you have not forgotten her, and that you will come back and visit often.

6. Take a few deep breaths and end the exercise. You may utilize today's writing space in one of two ways. You might, as usual, record your impressions of the experience. Or you might let your Inner Child do the writing. This is done most easily by holding your pen in your nondominant hand, making your mind a blank, and letting the Inner Child write or draw whatever she wants.

Month 1

Month 3

Month 4

Month 5

Month ☼:

Day 5

Forgiveness

TIME REQUIRED: *as long as necessary*

Forgiveness—of ourselves and others—is one of the most powerful tools of growth and healing available to us. This exercise is a wonderful way to let go of old, outgrown hurts.

◊   ◊   ◊

1. Get comfortable and do the relaxation exercise.

2. Think of a person in your life whom you believe has wronged you in some way. Mentally put him/her in front of you. Allow yourself to feel anger at him for what occurred. Tell him how you feel, how he hurt you—tell him everything you think he ought to know. Get it all out. See the anger pouring out of you like black smoke.

3. Now let it go. See the black smoke start to fade and disappear. See it turning to white smoke, then to nothingness. Now say in your mind, "I forgive _____ for (whatever he has done). And

I forgive myself for having judged ____." Tell that person in your mind that he is forgiven. Now see yourself embracing him.

4. Choose another person, and do the exercise again. Keep doing it until you feel at peace.

Variation: If you are the person whom you feel most needs your forgiveness, this exercise works just as well. Place your own image in your mind and do all the steps of the meditation.

5. Write down your impressions of the experience in the space provided.

Month 1

_____

_____

_____

_____

_____

_____

_____

Month 2

_____

_____

Month 3

Month 4

Month 5

Month 6:

29

Prosperity

TIME REQUIRED: *ten to fifteen minutes*

There are precious few of us who could not benefit from raising our prosperity consciousness. This exercise is very useful in removing limiting blocks and opening ourselves to the abundance of the Universe. Don't be surprised if soon after doing the exercise you receive some unexpected sources of income!

◊ ◊ ◊

1. Get comfortable, close your eyes, and do the relaxation exercise.

2. Say to yourself, "I now release any beliefs I have that I need to suffer, struggle, or work myself to death in order to be prosperous."

3. Picture everything good that you want and need coming to you effortlessly and in perfect ways. Seeing it come "in perfect ways" signals the Universe that you are not seeking to benefit from the misfortunes of others.

4. Picture yourself enjoying your prosperity and visualize the people in your life, as well as humankind in general, greatly benefiting from your good fortune.

5. Affirm, "The Universe is abundant and generous. Prosperity is my birthright. I accept it now."

6. End the exercise, and write down your impressions of the experience in the space provided.

Month 1

_____

_____

_____

_____

_____

_____

_____

Month 2

_____

_____

_____

_____

Month 3

Month 4

Month 5

_____
_____
_____
_____
_____
_____
_____

Month 6:

_____
_____
_____
_____
_____
_____
_____
_____

Day 7

Changing Chairs

TIME REQUIRED: *five to ten minutes*

This is an old standby, and does it ever work. Its purpose is to help you resolve a problematic relationship by increasing your ability to see the other person's point of view.

○ ○ ○

1. Sit down in a chair, preferably a straight-backed one. Place a similar chair directly across from you.

2. Get comfortable, close your eyes, and do the relaxation exercise.

3. In your mind's eye, place the person you are having difficulties with in the chair across from you. See him or her clearly. Then, as if the person were really there, talk to him or her. Say what's on your mind. Ask why he or she did such-and-such. Give your point of view.

34

4. Now get up and change chairs. Pretend that, with the chair-changing, you have actually become the other person. Without judgment, very honestly, try to get into that other person's mind. Talk back. Answer those questions about why you did such-and-such. Say what's on your mind. Give your point of view.

5. Go back and forth with this a few times. Explore the issues and feelings that are brought up. Try to understand each other's point of view, and aim to bring the two viewpoints closer together. If you can't accomplish this right off, at the very least you'll have a new, deeper understanding of the other person.

6. End the exercise, and write down your impressions of the experience in the space provided.

Note: This exercise can be used not only for difficult present-day relationships but also to help resolve past conflicts. It doesn't matter if the person you mentally summon into that other chair has been dead for twenty years—you still can gain tremendous insights.

Month 1

_____

_____

_____

_____

_____

_____

_____

_____

_____

_____

_____

_____

_____

Month 2

_____

_____

_____

_____

_____

_____

Month 3

Month 4

Month 5

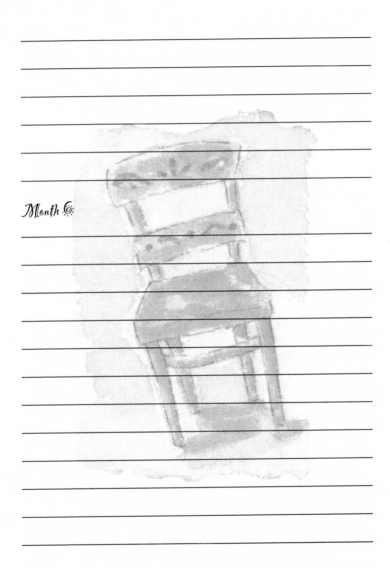

Month 6:

 *Day* 8

Kindness
Day

TIME REQUIRED: *ten minutes*

There is an old expression: "Do all the good you can, in all the ways you can, to all the people you can, at all the times you can, as long as ever you can." This is one of my all-time favorite meditations toward that end. It's a magical feeling to be Santa Claus for a day—and don't forget, you're helping yourself as well. What goes around comes around, and whatever kindnesses you do for others will eventually come back to you.

◊ ◊ ◊

1. Get comfortable, close your eyes, and do the relaxation exercise. Open your eyes.

2. In the space provided, make a list of people in your life, past and present. Family, friends, enemies, acquaintances. The more, the better.

3. Think of some lovely thing you can do for each one—a highly personal gesture or gift that

would really mean something to them. Perhaps an elderly aunt would enjoy receiving the latest snapshots of your children. Maybe your secretary would appreciate a surprise basket of flowers. Maybe your spouse needs to find a little love note on the pillow when he or she gets home. Maybe an old enemy needs an apology. Maybe a school chum you haven't seen for twenty years would like a call. The longer the list, the better.

4. Write down every idea you think of. If some of them require preparation, and today isn't the optimum time to have your actual Kindness Day, at least prepare the list as thoroughly as you can.

5. Either today or at the first available opportunity, carry out Kindness Day. Be Santa Claus. Do as many of the things on your list as you can. Any that you haven't time to do, do next month.

Month 1

_____

_____

_____

_____

Month 2

Month 3

44

Month 4

Month 5

Month ☼:

_____

_____

_____

_____

_____

_____

_____

_____

_____

_____

_____

_____

_____

_____

_____

_____

_____

_____

_____

 Day

Your
Probable Self

TIME REQUIRED: *ten to fifteen minutes*

The concept of a Probable Self—the you who could have been, had circumstances been different in your life—is a fascinating one. Some people believe that our Probable Selves exist as undeniably as we do, living in Probable Universes. Others see them as no more than fantasy. Whatever your belief, exploring the life you could have led is a worthwhile exercise. Not only does it enrich your own reality by letting you peer into another, but it also gives you insights into new directions you might explore!

◦ ◦ ◦

1. Get comfortable, close your eyes, and do the relaxation exercise.

2. Imagine yourself walking through a beautiful field. You come to the end of the field and find yourself looking down into a swiftly moving stream. In front of you is a bridge. The bridge is

entirely covered with a golden mist. You walk unhesitatingly through the mist. You know that on the other side you will meet a Self who is you and, at the same time, not you—a self that you could have been had you made different choices than the ones you made.

3. There, on the other side of the bridge, is your Probable Self. What does he or she look like? What is he or she doing? Where does he or she live? What is his or her family life like? Professional life? What choices did he or she make that were different from yours?

4. Ask this person why, of all the Probable Selves who could have greeted you, you chose him or her. What special message does he or she have for you in your life?

5. End the exercise, and write down your impressions of the experience in the space provided. Think about what your Probable Self might be able to teach you, and try to incorporate it into your own life.

Month 1

_____
_____
_____
_____
_____
_____
_____
_____
_____
_____
_____
_____
_____

Month 2

_____
_____
_____
_____
_____
_____

Month 3

Month 4

_____

_____

_____

_____

_____

_____

_____

_____

_____

_____

_____

Month 5

_____

_____

_____

_____

_____

Month 6:

Day 10

Love Letter

TIME REQUIRED: *fifteen minutes*

This wonderful exercise, adapted from Christopher's book, *Re-Creating Your Self*, is a powerful tool for improving your relationship with You and for giving yourself the love and appreciation you deserve.

0   0   0

1. Pick up a pen, and in the space provided write a letter to yourself—a love letter. In it point out all the things that make you lovable, and forgive yourself for any and all perceived shortcomings. Acknowledge that you are worthy of being loved, both by yourself and by others, and promise to treat yourself beautifully from now on.

Really have fun with this exercise. Don't feel shy or embarrassed—you deserve this gift of love.

Dear

_____

_____

_____

_____

_____

_____

_____

_____

_____

_____

_____

_____

_____

_____

_____

_____

_____

Love

Dear

_____

_____

_____

_____

_____

_____

_____

_____

_____

_____

_____

_____

_____

_____

_____

_____

_____

_____

Love

Dear

_____

_____

_____

_____

_____

_____

_____

_____

_____

_____

_____

_____

_____

_____

_____

_____

_____

Love

Dear

_____

_____

_____

_____

_____

_____

_____

_____

_____

_____

_____

_____

_____

_____

_____

_____

_____

_____

Love

Dear

_____

_____

_____

_____

_____

_____

_____

_____

_____

_____

_____

_____

_____

_____

_____

_____

_____

_____

Love

Dear

_____

_____

_____

_____

_____

_____

_____

_____

_____

_____

_____

_____

_____

_____

_____

_____

_____

_____

Love

Dear

_____

_____

_____

_____

_____

_____

_____

_____

_____

_____

_____

_____

_____

_____

_____

_____

_____

Love

Day 11

When You Wish Upon Yourself

TIME REQUIRED: *ten to fifteen minutes*

This exercise is a fun one—it's not often you get to be both a genie in a bottle *and* a master in one short meditation!

o   o   o

1. Get comfortable, close your eyes, and do the relaxation exercise.

2. Imagine yourself walking along a beach. At your feet you see an interesting carved bottle. You pick it up, pull out the stopper, and lo and behold, a huge puff of smoke comes out. A smiling genie appears before you and tells you that since you opened the bottle, you are his or her

master. "I will grant you any wish," the genie
announces.

3. Think for a moment, then tell the genie what
your wish is.

4. Now mentally change places—turn from the
master into the genie. Look objectively, from the
genie's point of view, at your own life and the
wish you have just made. All right, so maybe
you can't quite blink the wish into instant fulfillment, but ask yourself what can be done to grant
the desire. For example, if good health is your
wish, you might take a giant step toward grant-
ing it by breaking any unhealthy habits you
have. If you wished for a better job, you might
start attending night school to get a degree.
Make solid, step-by-step plans to help your master achieve his or her desire.

5. End the exercise. Write down your experiences
in the space provided and start making your
wishes come true.

Month 1

_____

_____

_____

_____

Month 2

Month 3

Month 4

Month 5

68

Month ☼:

_____
_____
_____
_____
_____
_____
_____
_____
_____
_____
_____
_____
_____
_____
_____
_____
_____
_____
_____
_____
_____
_____
_____

Day 12

Your Relationships

TIME REQUIRED: *five to ten minutes*

This exercise can reconnect you with the importance and value of your relationships, and can give you an opportunity to send powerful energy toward those you love.

๏ ๏ ๏

1. Get comfortable, close your eyes, and do the relaxation exercise.

2. Decide on the four most important ongoing relationships in your life. One by one, call each person into your mind. Visualize each loved one as happy, healthy, successful, and bathed in perfect white light. Take a moment mentally to thank each person for being in your life, and list all the qualities and memories you most love about them.

   (After the meditation, you may wish to call your loved ones up and say those same nice things in actuality!)

3. Now get more specific. Ask yourself what each person's favorite dream is, then visualize him or her having just achieved it. Has your father always wanted a red Corvette? Visualize him speeding around in it. Has your best friend always yearned to get her country and western songs published? Imagine her calling you up to say she's gotten a contract. Is your favorite uncle unwell? Imagine him totally healed.

Note: This exercise is not to be confused with Kindness Day (Exercise #8), in which you actually do small concrete things to enhance the lives of those you love. This is a purely mental process, sending helpful energy toward making the big dreams in their lives come true.

4. Take a few deep breaths and end the exercise. Write your impressions in the space provided.

Month 1

_____

_____

_____

_____

_____

_____

Month 2

Month 3

Month 4

73

Month 5

Month 6:

$\mathcal{D}ay$ 13

Get Out of That Rut

TIME REQUIRED: *five to ten minutes*

This is a good self-examination exercise to free you from any bad patterns you might be stuck in. Most of us are in some rut or other—a fixed routine of thought or action that limits our sense of creativity, dynamism, and fulfillment. It might be a minor rut—like having dinner with the same friend at the same restaurant every Wednesday night. Or it might be a major rut, like staying in a job you hate simply because it's comfortable. But major or minor, it's time to live consciously, not merely as a creature of habit.

ø   ø   ø

1. Close your eyes, get comfortable, and do the relaxation exercise.

2. Think about a particular rut you're in, one that you

feel you're ready to get out of. Ask yourself why you're in the rut in the first place. Was being there ever a happy experience? Did you choose it for a reason, or did it just sort of happen? How long have you been in it? Now ask yourself what would happen if you got out of it. Would you be uncomfortable? Scared? Triumphant? What would the price be for leaving the rut?

3. If you still feel you're ready to make a change, make a list of all the ways you could get out of this particular rut. If you're dealing with a minor rut, it's fun and easy to make the list. If you're dealing with a major rut, it may be more difficult to make changes. But keep with it, keep examining different possibilities, keep reminding yourself that you, not habit or circumstances, are in control. Eventually you'll get some momentum going.

4. Take a few deep breaths and end the exercise. Write down your impressions of the experience in the space provided. Now do something about getting out of that rut!

Note: We suggest that the first few times you do this exercise, concentrate on changing minor ruts. The more minor ruts you are able to change, the more self-confident you will become about your ability to have control over your life. Then, when the time comes, tackling the major ruts will be that much easier.

Month 1

_____

_____

_____

_____

_____

_____

_____

_____

_____

_____

_____

_____

_____

Month 2

_____

_____

_____

_____

_____

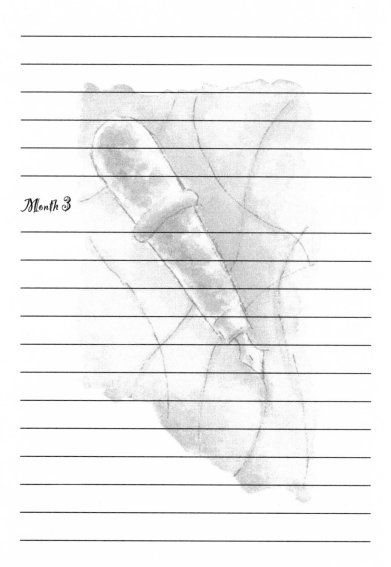

Month 3

Month 4

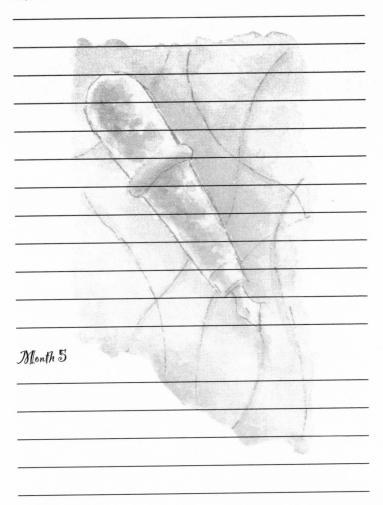

Month 5

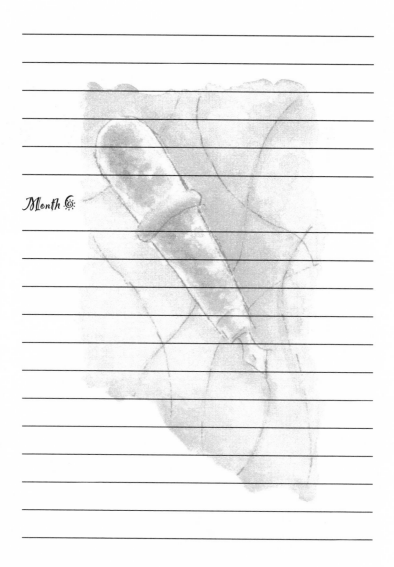

Month ☼:

Day 14

Affirmations

TIME REQUIRED: *ten minutes*

Affirmations are phrases or sentences that, when repeated either verbally or in writing, keep us centered in our best selves. The more you can write or repeat them, the better. Once a day is great, twice a day is twice as great. But a little is better than none, so we have included two affirmation days in our journal. If you can make them a part of your everyday routine, wonderful.

o o o

1. Take a few deep breaths, get comfortable, and do the relaxation technique.

2. Choose one of the following affirmations:

   Going Forth This is God's day, perfect and whole. I go forth to accept my expected and unexpected good.

   Safety I place an aura of divine protection and divine love entirely around my world. I am perfectly safe.

Health I am radiant with vibrant health. I feel more alive with every breath I take.

Abundance I am a magnet for all good things.

Love I am surrounded with the perfect, unconditional love of God. And I give this love to everyone I meet.

A Relationship or Situation That Needs Healing My relationship (or situation) with _____ is in the hands of God. It will work itself out perfectly.

Self-Worth I am a valuable human being, doing God's perfect work. I am grateful to be me.

And my all-time favorite affirmation:

I love my life! I love my life! I love my life!

3. Repeat your chosen affirmation, either out loud or silently, with joy and enthusiasm. Then, after several minutes, write down the affirmation as many times as you can in the space provided.

Note: Please feel free to write your own affirmations, to suit any needs you might have.

Month 1

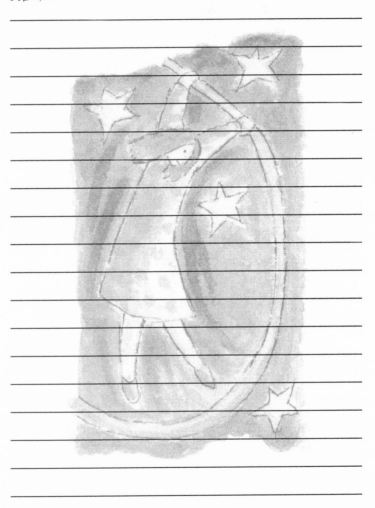

Month 2

Month 3

Month 4

Month 5

Month 6:

To Your Health

TIME REQUIRED: *ten minutes*

Health—that dynamic state of physical, emotional, and spiritual well-being with perfect bodily and mental functioning—is the single most important thing an individual can possess, next to life itself. This exercise will both help you maintain your health and help you heal if you are having a physical difficulty.

● ● ●

1. Get comfortable, close your eyes, and do the relaxation exercise.

2. Visualize yourself in perfect health. In your mind's eye, see yourself glowing with radiant energy, looking wonderful, feeling even better. Let that vision seep into your subconscious and become a fixed part of your ongoing reality.

3. If you are ill at the moment, ask yourself why. At a conservative estimate, over 90 percent of all

illnesses are in some way psychological or stress-related. Try to identify the underlying reason for your physical illness. Are you holding onto any negative feelings, any unhealthy attitudes? Have you any toxic beliefs that need to be released? Once you've identified these beliefs or feelings, you can work on letting them go. (The exercise for Day 18, "Releasing Your Feelings," will be very helpful toward this end.)

4. Now ask your all-wise subconscious mind what color light you need to get well. When you have the answer, send that color light to the area that needs help. In your mind's eye, see the light absorbed into your body, doing its perfect healing work.

5. End the exercise and write down your impressions of the experience in the space provided.

Month 1

Month 2

_____

_____

_____

_____

_____

Month 3

_____

_____

_____

_____

_____

Month 4

_____

_____

_____

_____

Month 5

Month 6

$\mathcal{D}ay$ 16

The Time Machine

TIME REQUIRED: *ten minutes*

This fun, imaginative exercise will help you focus on your life goals and what you can do to make them happen.

∅   ∅   ∅

1. Get comfortable, close your eyes, and do the relaxation exercise.

2. Imagine you are getting into a time machine that will take you twenty years into the future. Picture yourself entering the capsule, fiddling with some buttons, and presto! In only a few seconds you have moved ahead twenty years.

3. You emerge from the capsule. There to greet you is your Future Self. You are absolutely thrilled—the future You looks wonderful, is radiantly healthy, obviously prosperous, and seems totally content.

4. The two of you sit down together on a comfortable couch. "How did you do it?" you ask. "What have I been doing during the last twenty years that has brought about such fantastic results?"

5. Listen to what your Future Self has to tell you. Get step-by-step directions. Ask about specific issues that are puzzling you in your present life. See what your Future Self says about the way you should handle them.

6. Get back into your time capsule and return to the present day. Start putting into practice the ideas your Future Self has given you!

7. Write down your impressions of the experience in the space provided.

Month 1

_____

_____

_____

_____

_____

_____

_____

Month 2

Month 3

_____

_____

_____

_____

_____

_____

_____

_____

_____

_____

_____

_____

_____

_____

Month 4

_____

_____

_____

_____

_____

Month 5

Month 6:

Day 17

Thinking for Yourself

TIME REQUIRED: *ten to fifteen minutes*

Even in this enlightened age, it's sad but true that most people are still followers, not leaders. To a great extent, most of us largely accept our ideas about life from organizations and other people rather than defining reality for ourselves. It's a deadening, narrowing, and ultimately tragic habit. This exercise is useful as a reality check, to let you know just how much of your own thinking you are in fact doing.

● ● ●

1. Take a few deep breaths, close your eyes, and do the relaxation exercise.

2. In the space provided, make a list. List all the people and organizations in your life from whom you are currently getting ideas and taking advice: spouse, parents, friends, coworkers, churches, healers, lawyers, and so on. Now write a brief summary of the advice they give you.

3. Read over the list. How does it strike you? Are there a lot of people on it? Do you actually take all the advice given? Are you happy with the results? Then ask yourself, Do I listen judiciously to what others have to say, but then ultimately make up my own mind? Or do I let my life be run by committee? Obviously, there's nothing wrong with being open to good advice — within reason. Ultimately, though, no one should make up your mind for you.

4. Now make another list. On this list, write down all the people to whom you often give advice, and perhaps even "think for." Consider children, spouse, friends, students, coworkers.

5. Review this list. How does it strike you? Are you someone who's content to let other people think for themselves, or are you constantly compelled to "put your oar in" and influence people?

6. End the exercise. Make a commitment to do more original thinking of your own and to allow the people in your life to do the same.

Month 1

_____
_____
_____
_____
_____
_____
_____
_____
_____
_____
_____
_____
_____

Month 2

_____
_____
_____
_____
_____

Month 3

Month 4

_____

_____

_____

_____

_____

_____

_____

_____

_____

_____

_____

_____

Month 5

_____

_____

_____

_____

_____

Month ☼:

Day 18

Releasing Your Feelings

TIME REQUIRED: *five minutes*

So often in life, "the problem" isn't the problem at all—it's our stressful feelings about it that cause the real upset. Strong feelings can create such a smoke screen between us and reality that we lose all sense of clarity and control. This exercise can help you regain both.

o   o   o

1. Get in a comfortable position, close your eyes, and do the relaxation exercise.

2. Think of a situation that is bothering you at the moment. Do not focus on the situation itself, focus on the stressful feelings it arouses in you. Do you feel burning anger? Overwhelming grief? A listless sense of "I give up"? Whatever

it is, for a few moments let that feeling run through you. Let it have full play. Feelings are important, and they deserve to be heard. When it's had its say, thank it for sharing.

3. And now let it go. Visualize that stressful feeling as a colored cloud. See it actually pouring out of your body like steam. Feel yourself much lighter and happier and freer than you were before.

4. Now visualize a big beautiful rainbow-colored balloon coming down from the sky. It lands gently beside you. Visualize the mist of feeling going into the basket of the balloon. Now see the balloon lift up, up, up into the Universe, taking the stressful feeling with it. You wave good-bye, knowing that it will be lovingly and perfectly dispensed with by an all-wise Universe, causing no more harm to you or to anyone else.

5. Take a few deep breaths and end the visualization. Write down your impressions of the experience in the space provided.

6. To complete the exercise, you might also want to get rid of any physical stress that is still lurking in your body. To do this, stand in a doorway and stretch out your arms until both hands are touching opposite door jambs. Now push with all your might and let all the stress go.

Month 1

Month 2

Month 3

Month 4

_____

_____

_____

_____

_____

Month 5

_____

_____

_____

_____

Month 6

_____

_____

_____

_____

Counting
Your
Blessings

TIME REQUIRED: *ten to fifteen minutes*

This is the oldest trick in the book for getting out of the doldrums, and for good reason. It works. How often are we told to count our blessings, and how often do we actually and literally do it?

o   o   o

1. Get in a comfortable and relaxed frame of body and mind.

2. In the space provided, start listing all the blessings that are especially meaningful in your life. Be creative and specific. Instead of writing, "My good health," for instance, you might write, "The energetic way I feel when I'm on the tennis court." Instead of writing, "My children," you might

write, "The way my little girl tucks her head into my shoulder when she's getting sleepy."

3. Make the list as long and satisfying as possible. You might need to place extra pages into your journal for this. I hope you do! As you write, really let yourself feel the happiness that each blessing brings into your life.

4. Read over the list. Thank the Universe for bringing such blessings into your life.

Month 1

_____

_____

_____

_____

_____

_____

_____

_____

_____

_____

Month 2

Month 3

Month 4

Month 5

Month ☼:

Meeting
Your Guide

TIME REQUIRED: *ten to fifteen minutes*

Many people believe that we all have spirit guides—souls from a higher plane who are lovingly helping us through this incarnation. Whether you agree or dismiss the idea as figments of the subconscious, it doesn't matter. At the very least, this exercise will help you get in touch with deeper parts of yourself.

o o o

1. Get comfortable, close your eyes, and do the relaxation exercise.

2. Imagine yourself sitting on a bench in a beautiful park. You feel radiantly excited because you know that something wonderful is about to happen and that you are about to meet someone who will change your life forever.

3. Through the grass, someone starts to approach. You know that it is your Guide, that special

spirit who has been with you from day one on this planet. How old is he or she? What does he or she look like? You embrace, and your Guide sits beside you.

4. You know that any questions you have about your life, any concerns, can be honestly and lovingly addressed by your Guide. Ask anything you want. Listen to the answers. End by asking, "Is there anything special I need to know right now?"

5. Thank your Guide for taking such wonderful care of you.

6. Take a few deep breaths and end the exercise. Write down your impressions of the experience in the space provided.

Month 1

_____

_____

_____

_____

_____

_____

_____

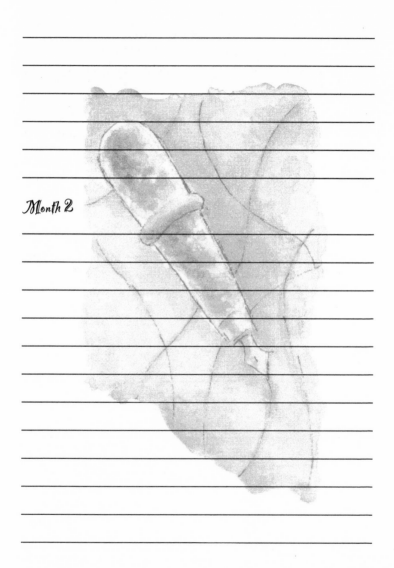

Month 2

Month 3

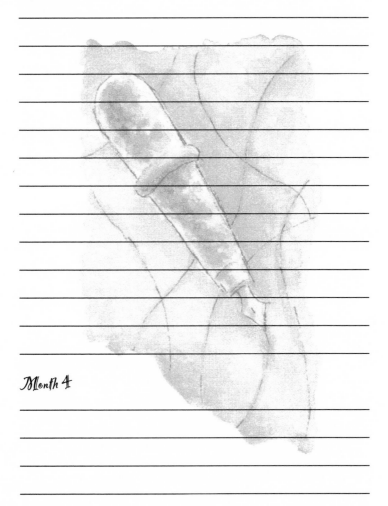

Month 4

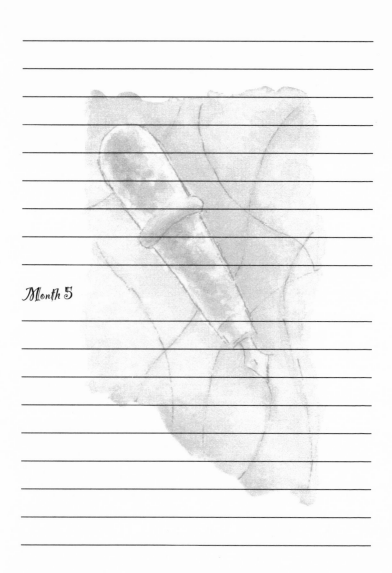

Month 5

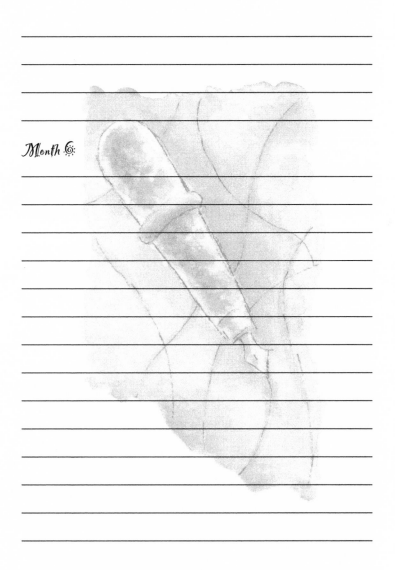

Month 6:

Day 21

Releasing Unhappiness and Accepting Joy

TIME REQUIRED: *ten to fifteen minutes*

Since this exercise has to be done outside, it may require a little preparation. But it's worth it—it's a lovely way to get centered and in touch with the rightness in all things.

o   o   o

1. Go to a quiet, peaceful place, and sit on the ground.

2. Close your eyes and do the relaxation exercise.

3. Feel the vitality of the earth—its electrical energy is dynamic life. Really connect with it. Be it.

4. Ask yourself this question: *Why am I not happy?* Then say aloud, "God within me, come forward. Divine Knowingness, manifest now."

5. Ask yourself again: *Why am I not happy?* Embrace whatever answer comes to mind. When we can really embrace and accept whatever challenges come into our life and see them as being there for our higher good—to help us grow, to teach us a karmic lesson—we can allow ourselves to experience the flip side of unhappiness, a release into joy.

6. Accept your challenges with gratitude and awe. They are your perfect teachers, sent into your life to help you reach the next level of development. Thank them.

7. End the exercise, open your eyes, and write your impressions of the experience in the space provided.

Month 1

_____

_____

_____

_____

_____

_____

Month 2

_____
_____
_____
_____
_____
_____
_____

Month 3

_____
_____
_____
_____
_____
_____

Month 4

_____
_____
_____
_____

Month 5

Month 6:

The Fork in the Road

TIME REQUIRED: *fifteen to twenty minutes*

This is a wonderful exercise for getting in touch with your wise subconscious mind and allowing it to help you out with decisions you need to make.

● ● ●

1. Get comfortable, close your eyes, and do the relaxation exercise.

2. Think of an area in your life in which a decision, large or small, needs to be made. Identify several different options you could take. (An example: you are thinking of changing jobs. Should you open the model train store you've always dreamed of, go back to school and get a business degree, or go to work for your father-in-law?)

3. Imagine yourself walking down a lovely little country lane on a spring day. Feel the wind, hear the birds around you. Now see yourself coming to

a fork in the road. This is a magical fork, the fork of your possible futures. Its purpose is to give you a preview of what your life would be like, depending on which decision you make now.

(Using the example above, the first path would represent what your life would be like if you opened the model train store, the second path would represent what your life would be like if you went back to business school, and the third path would represent your life if you joined forces with your father-in-law.)

One by one, follow each different path in your imagination. See where each leads you. Really let yourself explore what each possible scenario of the future feels like. Imagine yourself living out the experience. Would you be happy? What challenges arise? Is it worth overcoming them? Does the fork feel right, or does it seem like a dead-end? Let your all-knowing subconscious mind tell you which path is the right one for you.

4. Take a few deep breaths, thank your subconscious for its help, and end the exercise. Write down your impressions in the space provided.

Note: This exercise is equally useful in less life-changing decisions than the one in our example. It can even help you decide where to have lunch!

Month 1

_____

_____

_____

_____

_____

_____

_____

_____

_____

_____

_____

_____

Month 2

_____

_____

_____

_____

_____

Month 3

Month 4

_____

_____

_____

_____

_____

_____

_____

_____

_____

_____

_____

_____

_____

Month 5

_____

_____

_____

_____

_____

Month ☼:

Living in
the Moment

TIME REQUIRED: *ten to fifteen minutes*

We've all heard it a million times: in order to be truly happy and to live life most fully, we have to learn to live in the moment. We have to pay attention to and appreciate the instants as they pass. Very wise advice, but, if you're anything like me, it's very difficult to do. My mind is so busy racing along with past memories and future concerns that too often I barely notice the precious present moment at all.

This exercise is wonderfully effective in helping you focus. By doing it regularly, you can hone your powers of attention so that you can really start noticing what's around you and live in the moment.

◉ ◉ ◉

1. Collect twelve tiny but different objects from around the house and place them on a tray. Collect at random—a rusty nail, a chipped shirt button, a matchbook, a thimble, and so on.

2. Get a scarf or a kerchief.

3. Get comfortable, close your eyes, and do the relaxation exercise.

4. Cover the items with the scarf or kerchief, and wait one minute.

5. Remove the scarf, and for the next thirty seconds observe the twelve objects.

6. Cover the collection again. This time, in the space provided, write down as many of the twelve objects as you remember. Describe each object as fully as possible.

7. Uncover the tray and check to see how many of the objects you identified, and note how full and accurate your descriptions were. See if you can improve your statistics month by month.

Note: You can use a version of this exercise throughout the day, whenever you feel that your mind is wandering and you're not paying attention to the present moment. Close your eyes and ask yourself to describe some detail around you—the carpet, the pen holder in front of you, or any other item. Afterward, open your eyes and see how well you've done with your description. Keep practicing!

Month 1

_____

_____

_____

_____

_____

_____

_____

_____

_____

_____

_____

_____

Month 2

_____

_____

_____

_____

_____

Month 3

Month 4

_____

_____

_____

_____

_____

_____

_____

_____

_____

_____

_____

Month 5

_____

_____

_____

_____

_____

Month ☀:

Inner Voices

TIME REQUIRED: *ten to fifteen minutes*

We all have different psychological "voices" within us, talking to us and advising us every day of our lives. Some of the more common are the vulnerable Inner Child, the stern judge, the fun-loving hedonist, the fearful spoilsport, and the all-too-seldom-heard voice of intuition. These different sides of ourselves live in an uneasy truce, each clamoring for our attention. Sometimes their advice can be so conflicting that it's hard to make any sense of it whatsoever. This exercise will help you sort out those different inner voices and gather the nugget of wisdom each has to offer.

ø   ø   ø

1. Get comfortable, close your eyes, and do the relaxation exercise.

2. Think of an issue in your life that needs resolving. Know that you have an army of helpers within you who can assist you.

3. Now call them out, one by one. If you have trouble identifying your voices, you might start out with a few that everyone has—the Inner Child, the pleasure-seeker, or the stern judge. More voices might then suggest themselves to you. Imagine each voice as a distinct character. Ask each one what its advice is about your present situation. Listen to it talk. Do not try to censor anything; every voice wants and deserves to be heard.

4. When each voice has finished, thank it for sharing.

5. Now be very still and ask your highest self, your voice of intuition, to come forward. Listen to its advice most carefully of all.

6. End the exercise and write down your impressions of the experience in the space provided.

Month 1

_____

_____

_____

_____

_____

_____

Month 2

Month 3

_____
_____
_____
_____
_____
_____
_____
_____
_____
_____
_____
_____
_____

Month 4

_____
_____
_____
_____

Month 5

Month ☼:

151

$\mathcal{D}$ay 25

Last
Moments

TIME REQUIRED: *five to ten minutes*

At first glance this may seem to be a downbeat exercise, but it isn't at all. Rather, it's like Thornton Wilder's wonderful play, *Our Town*, in which the main character, Emily, experiences a brush with death and then recognizes the preciousness and the priorities of life.

⊘ ⊘ ⊘

1. Get comfortable, close your eyes, and do the relaxation exercise.

2. Imagine you are on your deathbed. You are in no pain whatsoever, but you have only a few minutes left on this earth. Your eyes are starting to fog over; you feel yourself detaching from your body.

3. You start to evaluate your life. What are your final thoughts about the way you've lived? What, in the last analysis, was really important

to you? Did you truly enjoy yourself on earth? Did you accomplish your dreams? What do you wish you'd done less of? More of? What are you proudest of? What are your regrets? Was there anyone you wish you'd been kinder to? Any loose ends that need to be tied up? Did you find your purpose in life, or did you miss it? If you had it to do all over again, how would you change things?

4. Take a few deep breaths and end the exercise. Write down your impressions of the experience. Take what you've learned on your imaginary deathbed and put it to good use.

Month 1

_____

_____

_____

_____

_____

_____

_____

_____

_____

Month 2

Month 3

_____

_____

_____

_____

_____

_____

_____

_____

_____

_____

_____

_____

_____

_____

Month 4

_____

_____

_____

Month 5

Month ☼:

Day 26

Past~Life
Recall

TIME REQUIRED: *fifteen to twenty minutes*

The idea of past lives is fascinating. More than half the world's population firmly believes that we have inhabited this earth before; other people find the whole idea ridiculous. Whichever belief you hold, this is a marvelous exercise. If you do believe in reincarnation, you can see this meditation as a way to get in touch with a past, forgotten self. And if you don't believe in past lives, you can view the experience as a way to access interesting and enriching information from the subconscious mind.

❂　❂　❂

1. Get comfortable, take a few deep breaths, and do the relaxation exercise. (As this exercise will need to be done with closed eyes, I advise you to read it over a few times first to familiarize yourself with what you are going to do.)

2. Imagine that you are climbing a mountain, following a clearly marked path. You come to a

wide ledge on the mountain that looks out over a valley. There is a comfortable bench on this ledge, where you can rest. Sit on the bench. You feel excited and happy because you know that you are about to travel to another time.

3. The valley below you is filled with fog. You are just above the cloud line, and as you look over the clouds you see a rainbow, its ends hidden in the clouds.

4. Stand up and fly out to the rainbow. It will safely support your weight. Step onto it and slide down into the fog, all the way to the bottom.

5. You have landed. Now look around. What do you see? Look at yourself. What are you wearing on your feet? What is your clothing like? What is your name? What is your age? Your occupation? What year is it? Where is home for you?

6. Go to that home. What is it like? Who lives with you? What are their names? What are they like?

7. Now move ahead in time ten years. Where are you now? What do you look like? What is happening in your life?

8. Move ahead to the end of your life — to the day you die. What is happening?

9. Move ahead to the moment of death. What is happening? What is the death experience like?

10. Notice that there is a door nearby. Go through it. You will see a flight of stairs. Go up them. By the time you reach the top, you will have left that past life and time behind you. At the top of the stairs, another door opens onto the mountain ledge where the bench is.

11. Rest on the bench for a moment, then descend the mountain path. Open your eyes.

12. Write down your impressions of the experience in the space provided. Think about your travels and why you chose to relive this particular past life. What is its relevance to your present life? How can it enrich or inform your present circumstances? Use what you have learned.

Month 1

_____

_____

_____

_____

_____

_____

_____

Month 2

Month 3

Month 4

Month 5

Month ☼:

Day 27

World Peace

TIME REQUIRED: *five to ten minutes*

World peace, or the lack of it, will be decided by the personal choices each of us makes. If you want to take part in creating world peace, your first and most meaningful step is to create peace within yourself.

❂ ❂ ❂

1. Get comfortable, close your eyes, and do the relaxation exercise.

2. Think about something that is keeping you from having peace of mind. Perhaps you have a relationship that needs healing. Maybe there is a fear that needs to be faced. Perhaps there is some personal or professional challenge you need to overcome.

3. Make a promise to yourself to change that situation. Vow to face that fear, overcome that challenge, or do your best to heal that relationship.

4. Visualize yourself standing in an open field. See white beams of pure peace originating within you. Watch them shoot from you in all directions. Feel the peace wash over you, warm and comforting. Now visualize those beams of peace extending farther and farther, like ripples in a pond. See them gradually covering the entire planet with their soft, healing light. Hold this image. Add other images that symbolize world peace to you—perhaps people of different nations and races holding hands, nuclear warheads being dismantled, people walking down the street smiling.

5. End the exercise and write down your impressions of the experience in the space provided.

Month 1

Month 2

Month 3

_____
_____
_____
_____
_____
_____
_____
_____
_____
_____
_____
_____

Month 4

_____
_____
_____
_____
_____

Month 5

Month 6:

Day 28

Affirmations
Two

TIME REQUIRED: *ten minutes*

Here's a second chance to do affirmations.

o o o

1. Take a few deep breaths, get comfortable, and do the relaxation technique.

2. Choose one of the following affirmations:

   Going Forth This is God's day, perfect and whole. I go forth to accept my expected and unexpected good.

   Safety I place an aura of divine protection and divine love entirely around my world. I am perfectly safe.

   Health I am radiant with vibrant health. I feel more alive with every breath I take.

   Abundance I am a magnet for all good things.

Love I am surrounded with the perfect, unconditional love of God. And I give this love to everyone I meet.

A Relationship or Situation That Needs Healing My relationship (or situation) with _____ is in the hands of God. It will work itself out perfectly.

Self-Worth I am a valuable human being, doing God's perfect work. I am grateful to be me.

And my all-time favorite affirmation:

I love my life! I love my life! I love my life!

3. Repeat your chosen affirmation, either out loud or silently, with joy and enthusiasm. Then, after several minutes, write down the affirmation as many times as you can in the space provided.

Note: Please feel free to write your own affirmations, to suit any needs you might have.

Month 1

_____

_____

_____

_____

Month 2

Month 3

Month 4

Month 5

Month ☼:

PART II

The Alternates

 Alternate **1**

Dream Work

TIME REQUIRED: *five minutes before bedtime; ten minutes upon awakening*

Dream work is a whole world unto itself. Many people passionately believe in its value; they keep dream journals, analyze dream symbols, and so on. This exercise is for beginners—people who would like to start exploring the fascinating world of dreams, which can provide help and guideposts for your waking life.

◊   ◊   ◊

To Be Done Right Before Sleep

Relax, take a few deep breaths. As you feel yourself drifting off to sleep, think of a situation in your life that needs clarifying or healing. Say to your subconscious, "Send me information about this in my dream." Keep repeating this until you sleep.

To Be Done Right After Awakening

In as much detail as possible, try to remember your dreams of the night before. Write down whatever you recall in the space provided. Now apply what you dreamed to the situation currently facing you. Did your dreams provide any help, any answers?

This exercise takes a lot of patience, so don't be discouraged if your dream work goes slowly. It takes a lot of practice to remember dreams in any detail, and sometimes the subconscious seems to take a long while to give answers. Keep trying!

Month 1

_____

_____

_____

_____

_____

_____

_____

_____

_____

_____

_____

_____

_____

Month 2

Month 3

Month 4

Month 5

Month ☼:

Alternate 2

Telepathic Communication

TIME REQUIRED: *fifteen minutes*

For those of you interested in developing your psychic powers, this exercise will prove very helpful. You'll need a partner for this one.

0   0   0

1. Get a pencil and a piece of paper for both yourself and your partner. Decide which one will be the Sender, which the Receiver. (For ease in explaining the exercise, let's make you the Sender.)

2. Go into a room without the Receiver.

3. Get comfortable, close your eyes, and do the relaxation exercise.

4. Draw a simple picture on the piece of paper, and hold the image of what you have drawn clearly in your mind.

5. The Receiver, meanwhile, should also be doing

the relaxation exercise in the next room. Keep sending the image of the picture until the Receiver feels he or she knows what it is. The Receiver should then draw the picture he or she feels was being transmitted telepathically by you.

6. The Receiver should then go back into the room with you. Compare pictures for accuracy and discuss the results.

7. End the exercise and write your impressions of the experience in the space provided.

Month 1

_____

_____

_____

_____

_____

_____

_____

_____

_____

_____

Month 2

Month 3

_____

_____

_____

_____

_____

_____

_____

_____

_____

_____

_____

_____

_____

_____

Month 4

_____

_____

_____

Month 5

Month ☺:

Alternate 3

The Spark

TIME REQUIRED: *one minute*

Do you sometimes get on a "negative bandwagon"? Do you find yourself obsessing on negative subjects? If so, this exercise will help you become more aware of your thoughts and root out the negative ones as soon as they come up.

❂ ❂ ❂

1. Get comfortable, close your eyes, and do the relaxation exercise.

2. Deliberately think about the one subject that makes you most uncomfortable. It may be a troublesome ex-spouse, an unpaid bill, a health concern.

3. Visualize that thought as a spark from a fire coming toward you. Watch it land on your sleeve and start to smoulder. You know that if you let it stay there, it's going to burn a hole in your sleeve. But if you can nip it in the bud, no harm will come.

4. Physically reach up and brush away the imaginary spark.

5. Think a happy thought to replace the negative one.

6. Keep doing this exercise religiously. Watch your thoughts during the day. See how many times that negative impulse keeps coming up, and every time it does, turn it into a spark, brush it off your sleeve, and replace it with a happy affirmation. Soon you'll be able to jump off the negative bandwagon.

Alternate 4

Five-
Minute
Pick-
Me-Up

TIME REQUIRED: *five minutes*

This exercise is wonderful for days when there simply isn't time to do the full ten-, fifteen-, or twenty-minute exercise. It only takes a few minutes and will fill you with a sense of peace and centeredness. Why not do it several times a day, every day, if you can?

◊ ◊ ◊

1. Get comfortable, close your eyes, and do the relaxation exercise.

2. Visualize the inside of your mind, and see it swept clean of all negativity by a golden broom.

3. Now visualize the golden God-spark within your

body. (You might see it located in your solar plexus or in your forehead.) See it grow and grow until it fills your whole body with light.

4. Now see that light continuing to shine, expanding and expanding until it touches everything and everyone you will encounter for the rest of the day.

5. End the exercise. Now go out and glow!

Suggested Reading

There are innumerable metaphysical/self-help books available. Here are a few of our personal favorites.

Psychological and Self-Help Books

Re-Creating Your Self, by Christopher Stone. A wonderful blueprint for examining and improving your belief system.

Taming Your Gremlin, by Richard D. Carson. A quirky and thought-provoking guide to overcoming your inner critic and enjoying yourself.

Coming to Life, by Polly Berrien Berends. Original and profound observations by a counselor-philosopher. (For those of you who have children, her *Whole Child/Whole Parent* is a mind-bending must.)

The 22 Non-Negotiable Laws of Wellness, by Greg Anderson. Powerful and concise, this single volume could take the place of a whole shelfful of self-help books.

How to Be Happier Day by Day, by Alan Epstein, Ph.D. A cheerful, idea-filled, and positive book.

Loving Each Other, by Leo Buscaglia. This man knows a lot about love and loving, and he shares it all in this warm volume.

Simple Abundance: A Daybook of Comfort and Joy, by Sarah Ban Breathnach. An enchanting book helping women bring more joy into their lives.

When All You've Ever Wanted Isn't Enough, by Harold Kushner. A sensitive and compassionate book about coming to terms with life.

Ageless Body, Timeless Mind, by Deepak Chopra. A beautiful blend of Eastern and Western thinking.

Metaphysical Books

Seth Speaks, The Education of Oversoul 7, How to Develop Your ESP Powers, and *The Nature of Personal Reality,* by Jane Roberts. Brilliant books by the premier metaphysical writer of the twentieth century. We recommend anything by this visionary author.

The Betty Book, by Stewart White. Written in the 1930's, this is still one of the best books about channeling available.

Out on a Limb, by Shirley MacLaine. An engaging and approachable book about an outspoken and courageous woman's journey into metaphysics.

The Three Candles of Little Veronica, by Manfred Kyber. A weird and wonderful tale of karma and reincarnation.

The Quiet Mind, by White Eagle. Teachings by the wise and compassionate American Indian mystic.

Image-Work Books

Living in the Light and *Creative Visualization,* by Shakti Gawain. My only regret is that these books aren't published in hardcover. I've reread them so often that my softcover editions have fallen totally apart.

The Science of Mind, by Ernest Holmes. The founder of the Church of Religious Science, Holmes is one of the greatest and most influential thinkers of this century. We recommend any and all of his works.

Thanks, Bonnie